W9-AOX-780

TODAY'S
SPORTS
GREATS

# TIM LINCECUM

By Jason Glaser

**Gareth Stevens**
Publishing

Please visit our website, www.garethstevens.com. For a free color catalog of all our high-quality books, call toll free 1-800-542-2595 or fax 1-877-542-2596.

Library of Congress Cataloging-in-Publication Data

Glaser, Jason.
Tim Lincecum / Jason Glaser.
    p. cm. — (Today's sports greats)
Includes index.
ISBN 978-1-4339-5880-9 (pbk.)
ISBN 978-1-4339-5881-6 (6-pack)
ISBN 978-1-4339-5878-6 (library binding)
1. Lincecum, Tim, 1984—Juvenile literature 2. Baseball players—United States—Biography—Juvenile literature. 3. Pitchers (Baseball—United States—Biography—Juvenile literature. I. Title.
GV865.L535G53 2012
796.357092—dc22
[B]
                                        2011007155

First Edition

Published in 2012 by
**Gareth Stevens Publishing**
111 East 14th Street, Suite 349
New York, NY 10003

Copyright © 2012 Gareth Stevens Publishing

Designer: Michael J. Flynn
Editor: Therese Shea

Photo credits: Cover, p. 1 Ezra Shaw/Getty Images; p. 4 Rich Frishman/Sports Illustrated/Getty Images; pp. 5, 12–13, 19 Jed Jacobsohn/Getty Images; pp. 7, 23 Chris Graythen/Getty Images; p. 8 Brad Mangin/MLB Photos/Getty Images; p. 9 Photo File/Archive Photos/Getty Images; pp. 10–11 Collegiate Images/Getty Images; pp. 14–15 Greg Trott/Getty Images; pp. 16–17 Brad Mangin/Sports Illustrated/Getty Images; pp. 20–21 Robert Meggers/Getty Images; pp. 24, 29 Christian Petersen/Getty Images; pp. 26–27 Jeff Gross/Getty Images.

Printed in the United States of America

CPSIA compliance information: Batch #CS11GS: For further information contact Gareth Stevens, New York, New York at 1-800-542-2595.

# CONTENTS

Words in the glossary appear in **bold** type the first time they are used in the text.

# CATCHING ON TO PITCHING

It all started with a game of catch in a backyard in Bellevue, Washington. Chris Lincecum was showing his 9-year-old son Sean how to pitch a baseball. Chris had been a fast pitcher in his youth but had injured himself. That inspired him to create a **technique** of pitching that delivered the ball over the plate at lightning speed, yet didn't tire the pitcher's arm. Younger brother Tim watched Sean practice their father's method. The motions seemed simple enough, so 5-year-old Tim copied the movements.

Chris Lincecum recorded all of young Tim's games and studied them to see how to make his pitching technique even better.

## Historic Family

Tim Lincecum is Filipino on his mother's side. His relatives moved to Hawaii from the Philippines in the early 1900s. They took part in key events in history, including a famous workers' **strike** in Hawaii in 1919. One of his uncles helped rescue American prisoners held in the Philippines during World War II. Lincecum is proud of his family's past and calls himself a Filipino American.

Sean and Tim both enjoyed learning the art of pitching, and Chris became their coach. As the boys got older, their father designed special exercises to keep their muscles both strong and **flexible**.

## DID YOU KNOW?

Timothy LeRoy Lincecum was born on June 15, 1984.

Few youth baseball coaches gave Tim a chance on the pitcher's mound because he didn't look like an athlete. It didn't help that Sean was much taller and more muscular. Sean made Tim look weak by comparison. Even when Tim earned his way onto the little league all-star teams, coaches rarely sent him in to pitch even one inning.

In Tim's first 2 years at Liberty High School in Renton, Washington, he played on the **junior varsity** baseball team. He began playing in the outfield since the team already had several pitchers. However, in his second year, he finally got his chance. By this time, he had learned to add **break** to his pitches. He immediately stood out as an ace.

## DID YOU KNOW?

When Tim Lincecum was a high school freshman, he weighed just 85 pounds (39 kg) and stood 4 feet 11 inches (150 cm) tall.

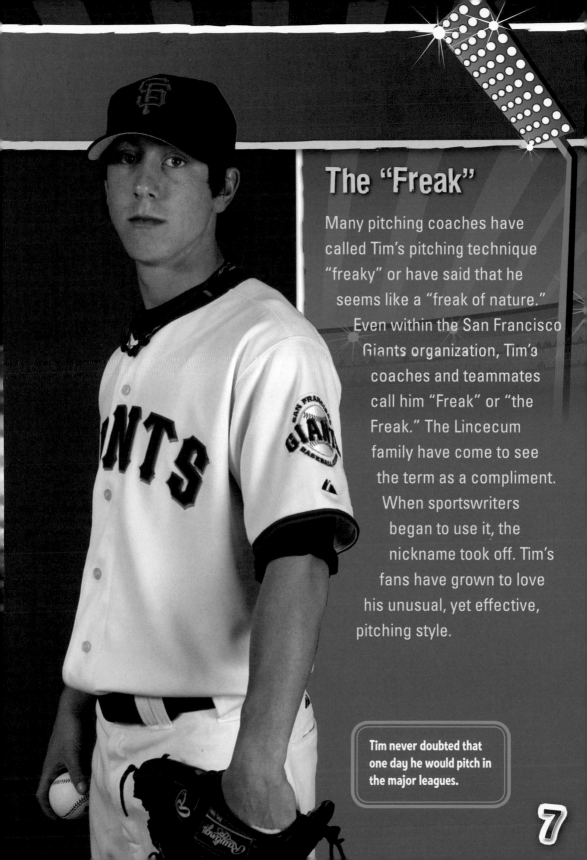

## The "Freak"

Many pitching coaches have called Tim's pitching technique "freaky" or have said that he seems like a "freak of nature." Even within the San Francisco Giants organization, Tim's coaches and teammates call him "Freak" or "the Freak." The Lincecum family have come to see the term as a compliment. When sportswriters began to use it, the nickname took off. Tim's fans have grown to love his unusual, yet effective, pitching style.

Tim never doubted that one day he would pitch in the major leagues.

Tim cemented a place on the varsity team in his junior year. With the bases loaded and two power hitters coming up, the coach sent Tim in to see what he could do. Tim struck out both batters to end the inning. The coach started using Tim as a **relief pitcher** because of that performance. He also got a handful of starts that year, earning four wins and two losses with an **earned run average** (ERA) of 0.73.

Tim Lincecum pitched the Liberty Patriots to the state 3A baseball championship.

In his senior year, Tim dominated as a **starter** with a 0.70 ERA. He earned 12 wins and led the team to a state championship. He was also named Liberty's Most Valuable Player (MVP) and given a place on the state all-star team.

## DID YOU KNOW?

Tim Lincecum recorded 183 strikeouts in 91.2 innings his senior year. That means he averaged two strikeouts per inning.

## Satchel Paige

Lincecum's homegrown pitching style is compared to Satchel Paige's. At a time when African Americans weren't allowed to play major league baseball, Paige was one of the superstars of the Negro Leagues. His strange pitching motions confused batters who were already unlikely to hit his blazing fastball. Paige often pitched all nine innings in a game. At nearly 60 years old, he ended his long career throwing three **shutout** innings for the Kansas City Athletics.

# MAJOR DECISION

Although 18-year-old Lincecum felt ready for the major league **draft**, the major leagues weren't ready to accept his unusual style. Lincecum was picked by the Chicago Cubs—as the 1,408th pick overall. However, a few colleges were very impressed with his high school career. The University of Washington was one of these schools. Lincecum decided to attend college instead of entering major league baseball.

Lincecum's college coach promised that he wouldn't try to change the young pitcher's methods. As strange as Lincecum looked, he got results with his pitching. In Lincecum's freshman year, he led the Pacific-10 (Pac-10) **conference** in strikeouts. The feat made him the first player in the conference to be named both Freshman of the Year and Pitcher of the Year.

## Amateur Leagues

College baseball isn't played at the same time as professional baseball. Summer is the prime time for pro baseball, while most college students are on a break from school. Many college ballplayers use these months to play for amateur summer baseball leagues. After his freshman year at the University of Washington, Lincecum played for an amateur team called the Seattle Studs and helped lead them to the 2004 National Baseball Congress World Series.

Lincecum broke many records as a pitcher for the University of Washington Huskies.

## DID YOU KNOW?

When Lincecum graduated from high school, his fastball was already 94 miles (151 km) an hour.

# TWO MILLION REASONS TO LEAVE

In 2005, Lincecum entered the major league draft again after a successful sophomore year on the University of Washington mound. The Cleveland Indians picked him in the forty-second round of the draft and offered him a $700,000 deal. Though it was much more than the draft position was worth, Lincecum turned it down. He felt he had talent worthy of an even better deal.

Lincecum's jersey number—55—was given to him randomly, but he liked it enough to let it guide his first car purchase: a Mercedes CLK55.

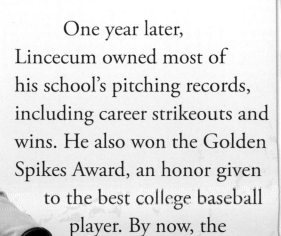

One year later, Lincecum owned most of his school's pitching records, including career strikeouts and wins. He also won the Golden Spikes Award, an honor given to the best college baseball player. By now, the San Francisco Giants were convinced. In 2006, they drafted Lincecum tenth overall and offered him more than $2 million. He accepted.

## The Major League Draft

Being picked early in the major league baseball draft is a huge accomplishment. In most professional sports, the draft has only a few rounds and a limited number of players. The pro basketball draft may have as few as 60 players, and the pro football draft may have around 200. In baseball, there are sometimes well over 1,000 players in the draft. In 2006, when Lincecum was the top pick for the Giants, 1,503 players were drafted.

## DID YOU KNOW?

Lincecum holds the record for career strikeouts for the entire Pac-10 conference with 491 in all.

13

# A MINOR DELAY

Like most drafted players, Lincecum had to prove himself in the minor league "farm system." The minor leagues train players and get them ready for the major league. Lincecum began in the Class A minor league by striking out 10 of 14 batters in four innings. After moving up a level for the rest of the 2006 season, Lincecum continued bewildering batters. Over six games, he struck out nearly 45 percent of batters he faced for a 1.95 ERA.

At the beginning of the 2007 season, Lincecum was moved up to the highest level in the minors. Even facing former major league players didn't slow him down. In 31 innings, he struck out 46 batters. By then, the Giants realized Lincecum's talent was wasted in the minors.

## DID YOU KNOW?

Lincecum is one of only a few minor league pitchers to have more strikeouts than innings pitched.

# The Minors

Baseball fans can see inexpensive, high-quality baseball by watching minor league games. Many players are trying to earn a spot in the majors. The lowest-level teams are in the "A" league. Players work their way up to "AAA" (or "triple A"). In triple A, promising young talent plays side-by-side with major leaguers who are working off **slumps** before returning to the majors. Major league teams replace injured or low-performing players with players from their organization's triple A team.

In the San Francisco Giants' minor leagues, Lincecum never pitched a loss.

15

Lincecum was called up to the Giants after another pitcher was injured. He pitched his first game for San Francisco on May 6, 2007. It was a mixed beginning for the future superstar. The first batter singled, and the second hit a home run. Lincecum recovered enough to strike out three batters that inning. Still, the Philadelphia Phillies hammered Lincecum to a miserable 10.38 ERA before the Giants pulled him.

Despite a poor showing for his first big league appearance, Lincecum received a standing ovation from San Francisco fans.

Even with his slow start, the 2007 season demonstrated Lincecum's strength. He averaged a strikeout per inning. His season ERA was a respectable 4.00. He also led all National League **rookies** in strikeouts. These were promising signs for a team finishing last in its **division**.

## Unwelcome Strikeouts

If there's one thing Lincecum could work on, it would be getting fewer strikeouts—when he's at bat, that is. In the National League, pitchers must bat like everyone else. Understanding pitching hasn't helped Lincecum become a good hitter thus far. In his first four seasons, Lincecum has struck out in nearly half his tries at bat. He's had three doubles, one triple, and no home runs.

## DID YOU KNOW?

Lincecum's first official win was on May 11, 2007, against the Colorado Rockies. He struck out six batters and allowed just three runs in an 8–3 win.

# YOUNG
# CY YOUNG WINNER

In 2008, Lincecum made the most of his first full year with the Giants. He continued his pace of averaging more than a strikeout per inning while also averaging less than one hit per inning. The result was the best win-to-loss percentage in baseball, with 18 wins and only 5 losses. He led the league with 265 strikeouts, 54 of which were made on just three pitches.

Unfortunately, the performances of the rest of the Giants weren't as good as Lincecum's pitching. They improved from last place to fourth place in their division but still had a losing record. Even so, Lincecum received the National League Cy Young Award. He was the first second-year player to win since 1985.

## DID YOU KNOW?

After winning his first Cy Young Award, Lincecum bought a French bulldog he named "Cy."

# The Cy Young Award

Each year, a Cy Young Award is given to the best pitcher in both the National League and the American League. The award is named after perhaps the greatest pitcher of all time. Cy Young pitched for a record 511 wins between 1890 and 1911. The award was first presented in 1956, a year after Young died. The voting is done by the Baseball Writers Association of America.

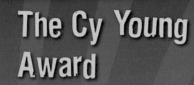

Lincecum's pitching coaches in San Francisco have left his pitching motion alone, with award-winning results.

**19**

The Giants began to build their team around strong pitchers. In the 2009 season, Lincecum was one of three Cy Young Award winners on the San Francisco team. He and Barry Zito had pitched together since 2007. In 2009, World Series winner Randy Johnson accepted a 1-year deal with the Giants. As good as the pitching staff was, Lincecum was the ace, leading the league in strikeouts for a second year.

Attendance at the Giants ballpark was over 3 million in 2010.

The Giants' batting efforts, however, were quiet. The low-scoring performance left the team at third place in their division, short of the playoffs. Despite the disappointing finish, the team showed promise of improvement. Lincecum was rewarded with a second Cy Young Award. He was clearly one of the keys to future success.

## The Bell

Some critics suggest Lincecum's success comes in part from playing in a "pitcher friendly" ballpark. The Giants' stadium—AT&T Park—is known as "the Bell" to fans because it's had several different telephone company names since 2000. The ballpark has several run-stopping features. Reduced wind flow and a high, distant wall in right field keep balls from being homered into San Francisco Bay—where fans hoping to catch a ball wait in boats with nets.

## DID YOU KNOW?

Lincecum led the league in complete games pitched with four in 2009. In one, Lincecum struck out a career-high 15 batters in a 4–2 win against Pittsburgh.

In 2010, Lincecum had the honor of being the starting pitcher for the opening-day game. He pitched seven scoreless innings for a win. This began a season in which the Giants would battle the San Diego Padres for first place. Such starts made postseason play seem possible. However, fans were anxious when Lincecum pitched five losses in a late-summer slump.

During a tight game against the Colorado Rockies on September 1, Lincecum finally snapped the slump. He lost only one other game the rest of the season. The Giants and the Padres stayed close until the very end. In the last regular-season game, the Giants beat the Padres to win the division and make the playoffs.

## DID YOU KNOW?

Lincecum occasionally does backflips for his teammates.

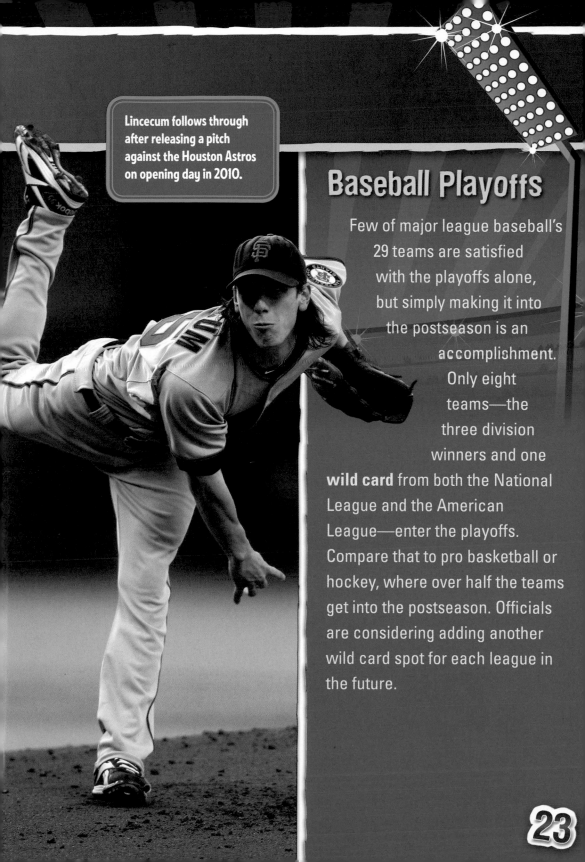

Lincecum follows through after releasing a pitch against the Houston Astros on opening day in 2010.

## Baseball Playoffs

Few of major league baseball's 29 teams are satisfied with the playoffs alone, but simply making it into the postseason is an accomplishment. Only eight teams—the three division winners and one **wild card** from both the National League and the American League—enter the playoffs. Compare that to pro basketball or hockey, where over half the teams get into the postseason. Officials are considering adding another wild card spot for each league in the future.

# WORLD SERIES CHAMPION

For his first-ever postseason start, Lincecum pitched a complete game that was a gem—a 14-strikeout shutout against the Atlanta Braves. However, Roy Halladay's no-hitter for the Philadelphia Phillies overshadowed Lincecum's feat. The two pitchers went head-to-head twice in the league championship series. Each got a win before the Giants advanced to the World Series.

Lincecum got the win in two of the four games needed to beat the Rangers in the World Series.

Lincecum faced the Texas Rangers' Cliff Lee in the opener. Fans expected a low-scoring pitchers' duel, but both men gave up runs. The Giants' batters helped Lincecum to an 11–7 win. When the two pitching aces met again in game five, Lincecum struck out 10 players in a 3–1 game. The Giants won their first World Series championship in over 50 years.

## The San Francisco Giants

The Giants began in 1883 as one of several New York baseball teams. As baseball grew in popularity, some owners hoped to make more money by moving teams to California. In 1958, the New York Giants became the San Francisco Giants and the Brooklyn Dodgers became the Los Angeles Dodgers, spreading major league baseball to the West. While the Giants' 2010 World Series championship wasn't their first, it was the team's first in San Francisco.

## DID YOU KNOW?

According to baseball **statistics** expert Bill James, Lincecum's shutout of the Braves ranks as the fourth-best postseason pitching performance in history.

# IN HIS FREE TIME

In his younger days, Lincecum liked to stay active. His restlessness existed even back in high school. While baseball was his favorite sport, Lincecum also played for his school's football, basketball, and golf teams. These days he mainly sticks to walking his dog to avoid being injured doing other sports. He lives out his other sports interests through video games.

Though usually happy relaxing at home, Lincecum enjoyed entertaining this crowd by doing tricks in a wind tunnel at a theme park.

Lincecum also loves movies and music. His close friends, most of whom are from his high school years, say he's like an encyclopedia of music lyrics. He always takes an MP3 player and laptop full of movies with him when he's on the road. Lincecum prefers watching movies at home on his big-screen TVs to going out.

## CHARITY WORK

Much of Lincecum's charity work is tied to his San Francisco life. He appears on posters promoting AIDS/HIV awareness in San Francisco, which has higher rates of AIDS than many other cities in the country. As a team based in an area with regular earthquakes, the Giants know the damage earthquakes can do. When one struck the country of Haiti, Lincecum pitched in for a charity auction to raise money.

## DID YOU KNOW?

Lincecum made his high school golf team even though he had played just 27 holes in his life before he tried out.

27

# TIM'S TECHNIQUE

The "freaky" delivery that gave Lincecum his nickname is the key to his game. Lincecum uses a distinctive long-stepping, body-twisting motion for all his pitches, making it almost impossible for batters to know what's coming.

Lincecum prefers his fastballs, either a blazing fastball with little movement or a fastball that breaks on the way to the plate. His change-up—a slower pitch that gets batters to swing early—has been almost unhittable, especially to batters still at the plate after a series of fastballs. He can also throw a wicked curveball for batters to chase. Since batters must wait to see the ball coming before they know what was thrown, they're often too slow to react. Then it's strike three!

## DID YOU KNOW?

Lincecum's windup isn't all about speed. His father's special technique puts less strain on his body, so Lincecum expects to pitch for a long time.

# Lincecum's Statistics

| Year | 2007 | 2008 | 2009 | 2010 |
|------|------|------|------|------|
| wins | 7 | 18 | 15 | 16 |
| losses | 5 | 5 | 7 | 10 |
| innings pitched | 146 1/3 | 227 | 225 1/3 | 212 1/3 |
| strikeouts | 150 | 265 | 261 | 231 |
| hits | 122 | 182 | 168 | 194 |
| home runs | 12 | 11 | 10 | 18 |
| walks | 65 | 84 | 68 | 76 |
| wild pitches | 10 | 17 | 11 | 9 |
| ERA | 4.00 | 2.62 | 2.48 | 3.43 |

**break:** a ball's curve from a straight path due to the way a pitcher spins it

**conference:** a group of sports teams that compete with each other

**division:** a group of teams located near each other within a league

**draft:** the selection of new players for a team

**earned run average:** the number of earned runs allowed by a pitcher, divided by the number of innings pitched, then multiplied by 9. The lower the number, the better.

**flexible:** able to bend without breaking

**junior varsity:** a high school or college team that competes at a level below the most skilled players, those in the varsity

**relief pitcher:** a pitcher who replaces another during a game

**rookie:** a player who is in the first year of playing a sport

**shutout:** a game or period in which one team does not score

**slump:** a period of poor performance

**starter:** the pitcher who takes the mound at the beginning of the game

**statistics:** a collection of numbers and data, or facts

**strike:** a stopping of work by employees as a protest against an employer

**technique:** a particular skill or ability that someone uses to perform a job

**wild card:** a place in a tournament for a team that did not qualify by meeting regular requirements

## Books

Dreier, David Louis. *Baseball: How It Works.* Mankato, MN: Capstone Press, 2010.

Eck, Ed. *Baseball in the National League West.* New York, NY: Rosen Publishing, 2009.

Rappoport, Ken. *Baseball's Top 10 Pitchers.* Berkeley Heights, NJ: Enslow Publishers, 2011.

## Websites

**Baseball Reference**
*www.baseball-reference.com*
This site is a great source for current and historical statistics for all baseball teams, players, and events.

**Giants Kids**
*www.mlb.com/sf/fan_forum/kids_index.jsp*
Young Giants' fans can learn about baseball from videos, games, and articles.

**The San Francisco Giants**
*sanfrancisco.giants.mlb.com*
Check out the official website for Tim Lincecum's team, the San Francisco Giants.

# INDEX